BE SILLY, BE DILLY, BE DOODLE, BE DOE THE BE ATTITUDES WE SHOULD KNOW!

JENNIFER FREUDENBURG

Copyright © 2022 Jennifer Freudenburg
Photography by Abi Schmit
Pattern by Nancy Halvorsen
All rights reserved.

No part of this book may be reproduced in any manner whatsoever without the prior written permission of the publisher, except in the case of brief quotations embodied in reviews.

ISBN: 978-1-63765-216-9
LCCN: 2022906053

Halo Publishing International, LLC
www.halopublishing.com

Printed and bound in the United States of America

This book is dedicated to my grandchildren: Caleb, Markey, Adelaide (Addy), and Micah, and to all the generations to follow. May they always be Godly leaders as they possess and live out His attitudes.

Prologue

In art, lines aren't always straight. Occasionally, they may even look slightly off-balance. That is sometimes a little like our lives, just a bit crooked and off-balance. There is beauty in that! Isn't it wonderful that we have a God who not only created us but deems us beautiful! He loves us every single day and accepts us, no matter how the art is played out in our lives.

See if you can find the  in each of the pictures!

Remember to  the attitude!

Be warm, be cozy, be snug, be safe.
Be silly, be dilly, be doodle, be doe.
Be God's caregiver wherever you go.

Some go to bed, shivering and cold.
A night of quivering is foretold.
A hat, a scarf, some mittens will do,
For an attitude of be warm you can pursue.

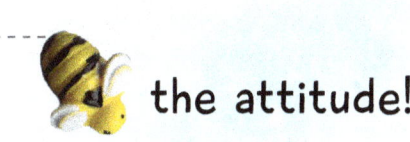 the attitude!

Why would a snow person be concerned about helping others stay warm? What could you do to help others who are cold? What have you done to show others you care? How has someone helped you this week?

Hints: Give a hat, gloves, or a scarf to a homeless person. Help serve a warm meal to those in need. Sew a small quilt from scrap material you have. What other ideas do you have?

Be loving, be tender, be hug-a-day daring.
Be silly, be dilly, be doodle, be doe.
Be God's comforter wherever you go.

Sometimes people hurt others and are mean.
They bully, they push, and they want to be seen.
Be loving and try to understand
What makes them need the upper hand.

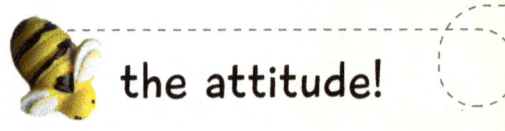 the attitude!

Why is the angel carrying a heart? How did you show someone love this week? How did someone show you love this week?

Hints: Share a smile. Share your lunch. Help at home with the dishes. Pray for those who hurt you. What other ideas do you have?

Be positive, be helpful, be useful, be sure.
Be silly, be dilly, be doodle, be doe.
Be God's example wherever you go!

Be positive in creating a happy place;
It tends to put a smile on a face.
When you are upbeat and think the best,
The negative thoughts are put to rest.

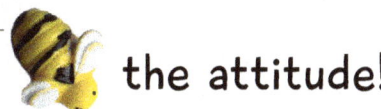 the attitude!

What does an ant carrying a cupcake on its back have to do with being positive? Can an ant really carry a cupcake? When was it hard this week to be positive? Why was it hard? How does being positive help make things better? How were you a good example to others?

Hints: Ask people how they are doing. Smile at people. Find something good in every situation. What other ideas do you have?

Be kind, be nice, be gentle, be caring.
Be silly, be dilly, be doodle, be doe.
Be God's goodwill wherever you go!

Be kind with the words and actions you perform.
You are God's ambassador, and this is your norm.
Be caring and gentle and go out of your way
To be the goodwill in what you do and say.

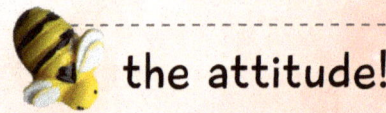 the attitude!

How is the bunny being kind? Share how someone was kind to you this week. How were you kind to someone this week?

Hints: Sharing the larger half of your candy bar with someone. Letting others go ahead of you. What other ideas do you have?

Be patient, be diligent, be willing to wait.
Be silly, be dilly, be doodle, be doe.
Be God's helper wherever you go!

Be patient, be patient, don't be in such a hurry!
To be calm and diligent causes less worry.
Be patient to lift someone's self-esteem.
In times of self-doubt, on you they can lean.

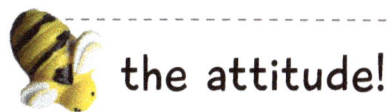 the attitude!

How is this girl showing patience? How did someone show patience to you today? How did you make things better by showing someone patience?

Hints: Practice having patience when you want something right away. Take a deep breath and count to ten when you need to slow down. What other ideas do you have?

Be respectful, be accepting, be reverent, be kind.
Be silly, be dilly, be doodle, be doe.
Be God's tenderness wherever you go!

To be respected is an honorable gift.
It gives others a kind boost and a lift.
They feel cherished and heard for who they are.
The sense of acceptance is overwhelming by far.

 the attitude!

How is the grandpa showing respect to the grandson? How could the grandson be showing respect to his grandpa? When you show respect to someone, how does it help? How have you shown respect to someone this week?

Hints: Being quiet and listening when someone is speaking. Standing up and giving an older person your seat. What other ideas do you have?

Be honest, be truthful, be ever so useful.
Be silly, be dilly, be doodle, be doe.
Be God's forgiver wherever you go!

In little and much, the truth must be told.
It is a Godly attribute to behold.
Don't lie, don't steal, don't try to deceive.
Being honest is your goal to achieve.

 the attitude!

How does this picture show someone being honest? How does it help us think of honesty?

Has there been someone you have not been honest with recently? Is it hard to tell the truth when you know you have done something wrong?

Hints: Say the words "I forgive you" when needed. Don't let a lie hang on your heart; confess it right away. What other ideas do you have?

Be prayerful, be blessed, be believing the best.
Be silly, be dilly, be doodle, be doe.
Be God's worshipper wherever you go!

God asks us to talk with Him every day.
It is up to us what we want to say.
We adore, we confess, we thank, and we ask.
We open our hearts to take off our masks.

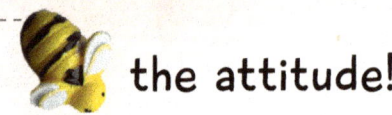 the attitude!

How does this picture remind you of praying? What are you praying for today? What would you want others to pray for you about? Where else can you pray, other than just at home?

Hints: Pray using ACTS:

A is for Adore	Dear God, you are awesome.
C is for Confess	Dear God, I'm sorry for what I did wrong.
T is for Thanksgiving	Dear God, thank you for the sunshine today.
S is for Supplication	Dear God, please help my mother feel better.
	What other ideas do you have?

Be smart, be sharp, be watchful, be alert.
Be silly, be dilly, be doodle, be doe.
Be God's devoted wherever you go!

Be alert, be watchful, be careful what you do,
For Satan roams, trying his best tricks on you.
Be smart and devoted to your God all around.
He sends His angels to keep your heart safe and sound.

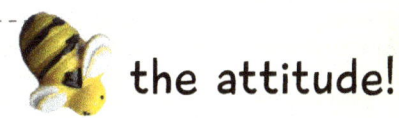 the attitude!

Why is it important for owls to be alert? Why are owls called smart or wise? When was a time you were smart by thinking something through and doing the right thing? Can you think of someone else who acted smart or wise?

Hints: You see someone dropping something without realizing it, and you pick it up and hand it back. You watch and listen before you speak or react. What other ideas do you have?

Be forgiving, be thoughtful, be patient, be true.
Be silly, be dilly, be doodle, be doe.
Be God's leader wherever you go!

God forgives you for all you do wrong.
He asks you to be His grace prints all day long.
You must be a leader all through your life.
To be forgiving certainly cuts down on strife.

 the attitude!

What does this picture have to do with forgiveness? When have you forgiven someone? Was it hard? When has someone forgiven you? Did it make you feel better?

Hints: Not holding a grudge. Not trying to get even. Saying "I'm sorry" and meaning it. What other ideas do you have?

Be grateful, be thankful, be pleasing, be glad.
Be silly, be dilly, be doodle, be doe.
Be God's goodness wherever you go!

Think of the good things given to you.
The weather, the water, toys old and new.
Be grateful to God for the blessings He does pour.
In thankfulness to Him, your heart graciously soars.

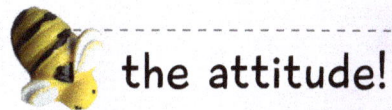 the attitude!

What are the good things you see in this picture? What are the good things you shared with others this week? What are the good things that have been given you this week that you can be thankful for?

Hints: Give it forward. Return an act of kindness. Thank five different people this week. What other ideas do you have?

Be joyful, be happy, be cheerful, be bright.
Be silly, be dilly, be doodle, be doe.
Be God's light wherever you go!

When you are joyful and happy and bright,
The world seems fresh and full of light.
Be happy going through life each day.
Then, at God's throne, your worries will lay.

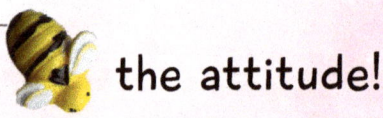 the attitude!

How does this picture show joy? What about Christmas brings you happiness? How have you brought joy to someone this week? How has someone shown you joy this week?

Hints: Share kind words. Offer a gift. Smile often. What other ideas do you have?

To the Earth, Jesus came as a tiny child.
In the manger, He lay so meek and mild.

He lived the be attitudes perfectly
To be God's example for all to see.

His mission to forgive and save was a must,
So He died and came back to life just for us!

Through His grace, heaven will be our home
To live in peace and harmony and never alone.

To God be all glory and honor and praise.
With hands and voices, exultation we raise!